HUNT EMERSON

CALCULUS CAT

Calculus Cat © 2014 by Hunt Emerson

Published by Knockabout Limited
42c Lancaster Road London W11 1QR United Kingdom

A CIP catalogue record for this book is available from the British Library.
Thanks to all the Kickstarter Pledgees.
Print edition ISBN 9780861662388
Digital edition ISBN 9780861662395
www.knockabout.com
Printed in China
First printing October 2014

Calculus Cat first appeared as a doodle, drawn sometime in 1978 while I was on the phone. The running, grinning cat was a nice repeatable shape that I could draw whilst semi-conscious – my preferred state. He acquired a name. At first it was going to be Copernicus Cat, as I was reading about the introverted astronomer-genius at the time, but somehow it changed to Calculus Cat. It rolls off the tongue more easily. The first Calculus Cat comic was drawn for *Everyman Publishing* (USA) in 1979, right at the start of their career when the limit of their ambition was a series of 8-page A6-size mini comics. They asked me to draw one – I was number 10 in the series – and I came up with a six page story, a cover and a back cover. Because it was so small, I drew the pages with just two rows of panels, and filled the top of the pages with a frieze of the running cat graphic. The style of drawing was un-complex, too, to match the page size, and the "story", such as it was, was more or less made up as I went along. That story introduced the central themes of Calculus Cat's life: his relationship with his television in his home life, and his anti-relationship with the world in his working day. Variations on those themes have persisted through all the subsequent Calculus Cat stories.

In a way it's odd that I should write stories based around television. I am not a TV watcher, and haven't been since my teens. I am of a generation that grew up with one television in the house, and as a teenager I always had lots of things to do in my bedroom that kept me away from the family telly. Those things included drawing pictures, playing guitar, reading, making model kits, and listening to records, as well as the usual popular teen activities, but it meant that from around 1965 I watched less and less general TV. I'm not one of those people who can work with the TV on in the background, so as I got older, left home and became a cartoonist I spent most of my time drawing comics and listening to BBC Radio 4 (my preferred medium of entertainment). I've lived by myself for prolonged periods, during which I haven't had a TV in the house, but even when I'm sharing my life with others and there is a TV, I only really see it in passing. This is not to say that I'm totally ignorant – I will sit down and watch *Come Dine With Me* if it's on, and I think *The Big Bang Theory* is brilliant – but if I do watch TV I usually go to sleep. The last time I had serious involvement with the medium was in the 1950s and early 60s, when I was a fan of Western series (*Rawhide, Bronco Layne, Have Gun Will Travel, Cheyenne*), cartoons (*Top Cat, Popeye, FooFoo & GoGo, Huckleberry Hound*) and adventures (*Whirlybirds, Highway Patrol, Supercar, Circus Boy*), and these became the favoured shows of Calculus Cat.

Then there's Skweeky Weets. Calculus Cat's world was narrowed even further by the need for his TV to advertise the World's Most Inane Breakfast Cereal, giving rise to the arguments and fighting between them that seems to take up most of the comics pages. Writing these arguments became my favourite part of the Calculus Cat project; the bit that makes me laugh. I am a huge admirer of Ray Galton and Alan Simpson's comedy writing – *Steptoe and Son*, and in particular, *Hancock's Half Hour* – and that's what I try to aim for when scripting the bickering dialogue between Calculus and the telly.

I wrote ten stories up to 1987, when Knockabout collected them as the comics album *"Death To Television"*. The majority of them were first published by Paul Gravett and Peter Stanbury in their *Escape* comic magazine, but after that the publishing history became promiscuous. I've never shied away from re-using stories whenever possible, and they appeared in various Knockabout comics, and in several foreign collections (including a German edition which publisher Carlsen chose to call *Choleric Cat*, for reasons that were never fully explained). I started another story after the publication of *"Death To Television"*, but I think *Escape* was wound up then, and the story remained unfinished until earlier this year (2014). There was a single page drawn for a special edition of the *Comics Journal* (2003) in large square format, which has been re-jigged into three pages for the book you are holding. A good friend of mine, Paul Wardle, commissioned a story, which he wrote and I drew. Paul, and Graham Higgins (Pokkettz) have been my only collaborators on the character. I've drawn a clutch of other Calculus Cat stories in the intervening years, including one that is unfinished as I write this, and so there are a whole bunch of pages that weren't in the original album and appear here for the first time.

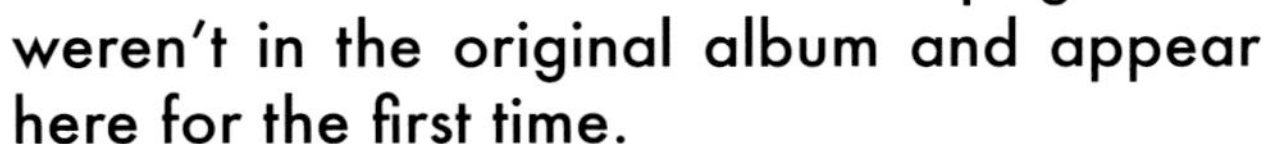

In 1987, at the time of *"Death To Television"*, TV was still fairly primitive and restricted in the UK to four channels. Video (VCR) was in its early days. Returning to Calculus Cat more recently has been odd. Digital, satellite, cable, view-again, flat screen, 3-D, freeview boxes – all these have crept up on me unnoticed, and made writing Calculus Cat much more complicated. I don't understand the new technology. True story – I recently had half an hour to kill, so thought I'd watch a half-hour's telly while waiting. Unusually, the TV was off, and – I couldn't even figure out how to turn it on!

We have published this edition of Calculus Cat using the Kickstarter scheme of crowd-funding, and we are hugely grateful to the wonderful people who backed the project and made it possible.

Hunt Emerson. July 2014

This photo of me, taken by my partner Jane White, is from around 1987, at the publication of "Death To Television".

CALCULUS CAT
HUNT EMERSON:
ENTER CALCULUS CAT, BEARING A TELEVISION...
DANSETTE
CHEZ C·CAT
FOOD
DING! DONG! DING!
HERE WE ARE- YOUR NEW HOME! AND THIS ROOM IS TO BE YOURS! FOR YOUR OWN! "THE T.V. ROOM!!"
MOTHER
Snif HMMMM...
T.V. TIMES
T.V. TIMES
OONOH·

SOMETHING IS AMISS?
WELL.... I DON'T LIKE THE DECOR IN HERE!

NO PROBLEM!! I SHALL REDECORATE THE ROOM IN YOUR OWN COLOUR SCHEME!! WHAT COLOUR WOULD YOU LIKE IT?!?

...I'D LIKE IT.... ...I'D LIKE IT....

...I'D LIKE IT THE COLOUR OF SKWEEKY-WEETS!

THE COLOUR OF SKWEEKY-WEETS?... WHAT ARE SKWEEKY-WEETS?
WHAT ARE..? ...YOU DON'T KNOW WHAT SKWEEKY-WEETS ARE??!!?
A SPUD

NOPE! NOT A CLUE!
Ooooh.... I feel faint! I SHALL HAVE TO TELL YOU THE FACTS OF LIFE....
WELL.... IT'S LIKE THIS....
DOOWAY

SKWEEKY-WEETS ARE SKWEEKIER AND WEETIER....
IZZAT SO?

NINE HOURS LATER....
...SO EAT AND EAT LOTS OF SKWEEKY-WEETS, THE SKWEEKIER WEET WITH THE WEETIER SKWEEK!!
...er...YES... ahem...er...I..er I REALLY MUST BE OFF TO..er... WORK...ah... heh heh......
CREEEAK-K-K
BLIMEY!...
DON'T FORGET TO GET SOME SKWEEKY-WEETS!
C. CAT Esq
GOOD MORNING, PUBLIC!
BLIMEY!! I HADN'T BARGAINED FOR THAT!! STREWTH!!
DAWN
WORK
NINE HOURS LATER....
WHAT A DAY! I AM BANJOED! BONKEROONED!! ABSOLUTELEY BLATTERED!!! ALL I WANNA DO IS FLOP IN FRONT OF THE TELLY AND WATCH SOMETHING GOOD! "BRONCO" OR "MAVERICK", SAY...
HELLO TELLY! D'YOU KNOW WHAT I'D REALLY LIKE??!
A BOWL OF SKWEEKY-WEETS? I KNOW JUST HOW YOU FEEL! THEY'RE SIMPLY FAB!
TREEYAY

NO... WAIT...
Y'KNOW, THE SQUEEK TO WEET RATIO OF THE AVERAGE PACKET OF...
HANG ABOUT! AREN'T YOU OVERDOING THIS SKWEEKY-WEETS BUSINESS? I COME IN BALALAIKA'D AFTER A HARD DAY'S GRIN... I WANT A LITTLE ENTERTAINMENT, BUT I DON'T EVEN GET A BLEEDIN' TEST CARD!..
...JUST ADVERTS FOR SKWEEKY-WEETS!!
YOU MEAN THE SKWEEKIER-WEETS WITH THE WEETIER SKWEEK?...
DON'T! PUSH! ME! TOO! FAR!!!
gulp OUR NEXT PROGRAMME IS... er..... er... "MAVERICK"!..
"MAVERICK"? GREAT!!
COMING UP RIGHT AFTER THIS IMPORTANT MESSAGE FROM OUR SPONSOR...
AAAAAARGH!!
SKWEEKY-WEETS ARE SKWEEKY AND WEETY!
I'M GOING TO EXAMINE THAT T.V. LICENSE FOR LOOPHOLES.... TOMORROW....
MAVERICK
PLUMPH
END
KWATROW

CALCULUS CAT
THAT'S HIM....
by HUNT EMERSON = (That's me!)

CALCULUS CAT, STRESSED AND WRACKED AS USUAL AFTER A LONG DAYS SMIRK, ARRIVES GRATEFULLY HOME...
THANK GOD FOR THAT!

HOW MUCH MORE OF THIS CAN I STAND? DAY AFTER DAY I SMIRK MY WAY THROUGH ABUSE AND VIOLENCE... NEVER A WORD OF THANKS...

...SOME DAYS I JUST LOATHE MYSELF... WHY DO I PUT UP WITH IT? I KNOW WHY- MONEY, THAT'S WHY! PSHAW!

WELL I KNOW ONE THING FOR CERTAIN- I'M NOT TAKING ANY CRAP FROM THAT T.V. TONIGHT! NO SIR!
IN FACT, I WON'T EVEN TURN THE DAMN THING ON!

HMPH!

CLI

AH! THERE YOU ARE AT LAST BOSS! I'VE GOT A LOT OF IMPORTANT ADVERTS FOR YOU TO WATCH, SO I WON'T WASTE ANY MORE TIME!...ahem...
BUY NOW WHILE STOCKS LAST!! BLUDKLAT BROTHERS BIG BIG, CAR SALE! SPEND! SPEND! SPEND! BARGAINS GALORE!!!
NO!! SILENCE YOU OVER-GROWN FISHBOWL!

I'LL HAVE NO MORE OF YOUR BLEEDIN' ADVERTS! I'VE HAD ENOUGH!
WHAT D'YOU MEAN YOU'LL HAVE NO MORE? YOU DON'T HAVE ANY CHOICE IN THE MATTER!
...EVERYDAY I DRAG MYSELF AROUND THE PLACE GRINNING AT THE GENERAL PUBLIC TO KEEP YOU HERE IN LUXURY....
YOU SIGNED THE PAPERS! YOU KNEW WHAT WAS INVOLVED!!

...WHEN I COME HOME I WANT TO BE SOOTHED AND ENTERTAINED BY MY T.V... NOT BE TOLD TO SPEND EVERY DAMN PENNY I EARN ON JUNK I DON'T NEED....
...IT'S NO USE MOANING AT ME! I ONLY DO MY JOB.... I HAVE TO SAVE UP ALL THE ADVERTS WHILE YOU'RE OUT, AND YOU HAVE TO WATCH THEM ALL WHEN YOU COME IN....
...ALL MY POTENTIAL WASTED ON THE RAT RACE, AND DO I GET ANY THANKS?? HO-NO! NOT A CHANCE!!
...YOU SIGNED THE CONTRACT... ANYWAY WHY SHOULD I BE GRATEFUL? D'YOU THINK IT'S MUCH FUN BEING COOPED UP HERE ALL DAY?!

GRATITUDE WOULD BE TOO MUCH AKIN TO MERCY, AND THAT'S ONE THING YOU'RE TOTALLY DEVOID OF, INNIT!? AND WHATS WITH THIS "COOPED UP"? YOU'RE A T.V. SET, FOR HEAVENS SAKE — WHEN THE POWER'S OFF YOU FEEL NOTHING AT ALL!
....YES...THAT GREAT HOLLOW NOTHINGNESS.... THAT DREADFUL VOID... MARKED ONLY BY THE ADVERTS SOFTLY ACCUMULATING IN THE MURK.......
...YOU THINK I DO IT FOR MYSELF? YOU THINK I GATHER ALL THESE ADVERTS JUST FOR ME?? NO — IT'S FOR YOU I DO IT!... FOR YOU!!
YOU'RE BREAKING MY HEART! REMIND ME TA SOB!! IF THE BEST WAY YOU CAN EXPRESS YOUR APPRECIATION IS BY BOMBARDING ME WIF STUPID ADVERTS FOR BENT CARPET TOUTS...
BENT CARPET TOUTS??? ...ARE YOU IMPLYING THAT I'M INVOLVED IN FRAUDULENT ADVERTIZING? YOU PIG!..... ALL OUR SPONSORS ARE GENUINE BUSINESSMEN OF THE FIRST WATER! HOW DARE YOU!!
TAKATAKA etc.
SHUT UP! SHUT UP!! SHUT UP!!! SHUT UP!!!!
ALL GOODS ADVERTIZED ARE OF THE HIGHEST QUALITY AND FAULT FREE AT THE TIME OF TESTING! AND MAY I SAY I'M GETTING REALLY FED UP SPENDING ALL DAY WATCHING ALL THESE ADS FOR ALL THESE CONSUMER GOODS THAT I CAN'T AFFORD ON THE PITTANCE YOU PAY ME!! WAAAAAHH!!
THAT'S IT! I CAN'T STAND ANY MORE...
HOW ABOUT A PAY RISE, YOU OLD MEANIE!
I'M LEAVING! IF YOU WANT ME I'LL BE IN THE CANAL!
4

SLAM!
GRRRRRR
WAIT A MINUTE! WHAT THE HELL AM I DOING OUT HERE!? FORCED OUT OF MY OWN HOME BY MY TV!??
GRRRRRRRRR
BOSS! BOSS! PLEASE JUST LET ME SAY ONE THING!
GRRRRR WHAT?!
IT'S TIME FOR WHIRLYBIRDS!
AWWW-GREAT!...
THE END

CALCULUS CAT
HUNT EMERSON
8-2002

THANK GOD- THE END OF ANOTHER DAY!
CHEZ -C- CAT

KAT -O- NOSH

KAT

AH-GOOD EVENING BOSS! TIRED AND STRESSED AFTER A HARD DAYS GRIN? WELL-RELAX! I'VE GOT SOME GREAT SHOWS ON TONIGHT!

BUT FIRST – DID YOU KNOW THAT SKWEEKY WEETS ARE THE SKWEEKIEST W...

YEEEEAAAAARRGGHHH!!

I DON'T GIVE A DAMN ABOUT SKWEEKY WEETS!! DO YOU KNOW WHAT IT'S LIKE OUT THERE? HAVE YOU ANY IDEA? THE SHOUTING-- THE VIOLENCE--THE BOTTLES AND BRICKS--THEY HATE ME OUT THERE, YOU KNOW!!

I RUN AROUND ALL DAY WITH THAT STUPID GRIN, GETTING INSULTED AND ATTACKED--I'M ONLY TRYING TO DO WHAT SOCIETY EXPECTS OF ME--AND DO I GET COMFORT OR SYMPATHY? NO WAY!! ALL I GET IS ADVERTS FOR SKWEEKY WEETS! WELL, I'VE HAD ENOUGH, DO YOU HEAR? YOU...YOU... WEEVILY YIPPING NICKNOODLE!

SPLATFACED ALIEN MUMBLETRUNK!... FEEBLE WIBBLING YAFFLETWANG!... BLOATED PIFFLING OATFIDDLER!... WARTY HUNCHED WOOFBLENDER...

SCABBY HALFBAKED CACKHOOTER... OH – WHAT'S THE USE...

...WEETIEST WEETY TREAT? SKWEEKY WEETS – BOTH SKWEEKY AND WEETY!
IS YOUR LIFE LACKING IN SKWEEK? SHORT ON WEET? HELP IS AT HAND! TRY ALL-NEW SKWEEKY WEETS TODAY!
THE SKWEEK IS WEETY AND THE WEET IS SKWEEKY, SO SKWEEK UP YOUR WEET RIGHT AWAY!
SO– FOR THE SKWEEKIEST WEET AND THE WEETIEST SKWEEK, DON'T FORGET THE NAME – SKWEEKY WEETS!
CLICK
AND NOW IT'S TIME FOR "MISSION IMPOSSIBLE"!
...your mission, should you choose to accept it...

CALCULUS CAT
HUNT EMERSON
HERE'S CALCULUS, ENGAGED AS USUAL WITH HIS "GRIN". BUT WHAT THOUGHTS STRIVE BEHIND THE FAMED FELINE'S REVERED RICTUS? LET'S TUNE IN AND FIND OUT.....
...PERHAPS IT WOULD BE SIMPLER TO GO MAD! THE WORLD IS HELL!...WARS, THE BOMB....OH AGONY...
...INSANE KILLERS ROAM THE STREETS.... TANKS AT THE DOLE.... EVEN THE LOWLY VEGETABLES OF THE EARTH ARE DEMANDING THEIR SHARE OF THE CAKE!! OH, MY HEAD.... NEARLY HOME AT LAST..... ≥SOB≤
WOSSONNER TELLY!?
PAH! SAME OLD DRIVEL! I THINK I'LL PUT ON A VIDEO!
HI BOSS! I'VE BEEN DYING TO TELL YOU ABOUT NEW SKWEEKY WEETS! THE SKWEEK IS WEETIER AND THE WEET IS.....
?
...SKWEEKIER! COSTS A LITTLE MORE, BUT THE VALUE IS MORE....er....VALUABLE! AND WHILE WE'RE ON THE SUBJECT- HAVE YOU TRIED NEW "OLD MA'S" OLD NEW STYLE OLD ROLLED OAT TOASTIES?
CLIK
THAT'S BETTER!

LATER...
...AND DON'T FORGET DICK DINNER'S D.I.Y. BONANZA THIS SATURDAY IN THE PUDDING DEPARTMENT OF THE JAMES MORIARTY FOOD EMPORIUM!
VIDEO
NOW WE INTERRUPT PROCEEDINGS FOR A NEWS FLASH.... REPORTS ARE COMING IN OF LARGE GANGS OF LOWLY VEGETABLES OF THE EARTH DEMANDING THEIR SHARE OF THE CAKE...
VIDEO
WHAAT?? OH NO- NOT AGAIN!!
EEK! PANIC!!
IT'S ONLY A FEW WEEKS SINCE THE FIRST TIME IT HAPPENED!...
CLIK RATTLE CLUNK LOCK CLICK
...I JUST CALMED DOWN AFTER THAT OUTBURST OF MILITANT LEGUMISM, AND IT'S HAPPENING AGAIN!! DOUBLE EEK!!
BANG
BANG
BANG
HANG ON, THOUGH... THIS IS A VIDEO RECORDING, INNIT... THIS IS THE FIRST OUTBREAK!!
SCREEEEEECH
HA! OH BOY! WHAT A SCARE! HOO! THANK GOD FOR THAT!...
WOW! I WAS WORRIED FOR A MINUTE THERE.... PHEW! MY HEART!
GOODNESS GRACIOUS ME!!
BOOM BOODY BOOM BOODY BOOM BOODY BOOM BOODY

HAHAHA.... "LOWLY VEGETABLES DEMANDING CAKE"... HEH HEH.... AS IF IT COULD POSSIBLY HAPPEN TWICE!...
SILLY ME! TEE HEE!... I'LL BE BELIEVING NEXT THAT THE VIDEO CAN ARGUE BACK AT ME, LIKE THE T.V....
NO YOU WON'T!
YES I WILL!
VIDEO
NO YOU WON'T!
YES I WILL!
NO YOU WON'T!
VIDEO
YES I WILL!! AND ANYWAY, EVEN IF MY VIDEO DOES ARGUE BACK, I STILL HAVE THE ADVANTAGE!
HOW'S THAT?
HA! BECAUSE WHEN I THINK OF A CLEVER RIPOSTE TOO LATE, I CAN REWIND THE TAPE AND INSERT MY WITTY WALLOP AT THE APPROPRIATE POINT!!
LET ME SHOW YOU! LET ME REWIND YOU BACK TO WHERE I SAID....
WEEDLEDEEDLEWEE
SILLY ME! TEE HEE!... I'LL BE BELIEVING NEXT THAT THE VIDEO CAN ARGUE BACK AT ME, LIKE THE T.V....
NO YOU WON'T!
GET KNOTTED!!!

HAHAAA! SEE!?!
BUT YOU'VE GOT IT WRONG BOSS....
YOU SEE, IT'S YOU WHO'S THE VIDEO RECORDING! -I PUT YOU ON EARLIER!
VIDEO!
THE REAL CALCULUS CAT IS STILL OUT IN THE WORLD, GRINNING- AND HE'LL BE HOME AT ANY MOMENT, AND I DON'T THINK HE'LL BE VERY PLEASED TO FIND YOU IMPERSONATING HIM!
Huh?
VIDEO
AND YOU CAN'T RUN AWAY, COS ALL I HAVE TO DO IS PRESS THIS PAUSE BUTTON AND......
VIDEO
IMMOBILE
GENUINE VIDEO PAUSE FIZZ
OK! ENOUGH OF THIS NONSENSE! I'M THE REAL CALCULUS CAT!
VIDEO
NO YOU'RE NOT-YOU'RE A BAD QUALITY PIRATE COPY!
I AM?
SUDDENLY...
CAKE! GIVE US CAKE!!
AND SO, DEAR READER THE OLD MONOPOLISTIC, CONSUMERIST, MEDIA-RULED SOCIETY IS OVERTHROWN BY THE WILL OF THE LOWLY MASSES.
—O—
AND, AS ALL COMEDIES SHOULD END WITH A CHASE.....

CALCULUS CAT

HUNT EMERSON

CHEZ C. CAT

CALCULUS CAT CAN'T SLEEP

TODAY!.... IT WAS NO BETTER THAN YESTERDAY.... BUT WAS IT ANY WORSE?

WERE THE ROCKS THROWN TODAY ANY HARDER THAN THE ROCKS THROWN YESTERDAY??

DO THE INSULTS OF THE PAST HURT MORE THAN THE BOTTLES OF TOMORROW??

OH GOD!! NOW I'M WRITING COUNTRY AND WESTERN SONGS!...

...HOT... THIRSTY...Glag... MUST GET A DRINK...

WHY? WHY IN HEAVENS NAME DO I CONTINUE TO SUBJECT MYSELF TO IT?!

CLIK

...'SCUSE ME.... SORRY TO DISTURB YOU... PARDON ME... ...'SCUSE ME...

I BLAME THE GRIN, OF COURSE... THE OLD IRRESISTABLE C.C. RIOTOUS RICTUS!
YOU
die

THE PUBLIC.... THE PUNTERS.... ARE HOPELESSY ENMESHED IN A LOVE/HATE RELATIONSHIP WITH MY GRIN....
GLOG
GLOG
GLOG

AND ME? HA! A SLAVE TO MY OWN SMIRK!

...SUPPLY AND DEMAND.... ...COMPULSION.... THE OPIATE OF THE MASSES...!TWAS EVER THUS....

BUT- MY INTEGRITY.... WHATEVER HAPPENED TO THAT? OR, GOD HELP US....

MY SOUL?!?

SIGH!!!
FLUMP

SIGH

I WONDER...PURELY OUT OF CURIOSITY, OF COURSE.... IF, AT THIS TIME IN THE MORNING.....

CLIK

WHAT THE HELL DO YOU WANT? DO YOU KNOW WHAT TIME IT IS?!?
OH, CHARMING! AND GOOD MORNING TO YOU, TOO! HMPH!
DON'T GIMME THAT! YOU'RE INDULGING IN A FIT OF MISERABLE SELF-PITY AGAIN, AND YOU WANT SOMEBODY TO WINJE AT, RIGHT?
CERTAINLY NOT! HOW DARE YOU!? MY VIEWING PATTERNS ARE MY OWN AFFAIR! IF I WANT TO VIEW AT...er...
THE TIME NOW IS EXACTLY 3:22am.
THANKYOU. 3:22am....
...THEN YOUR JOB IS TO BE THERE AND....
...AND...
...AND...
YES?
=sob!= OH GOD!! YOU'RE RIGHT!! I FEEL SO... LOST... AND EMPTY... I ONLY WANT TO CONNECT!...
ahem
BAWWW!

SPLAB
BLART
SNURF
SNUF
WiFFLE
...THERE THERE NOW... HERE, I KNOW WHAT YOU NEED—A NiCE, SYMPATHETiC-TYPE T.V. PROGRAMME!
AND OF COURSE, THAT'S WHAT i'M HERE TO PROVIDE!...
...SOMETHiNG YOU WANT TO ViEW.... TO FiT iN WiTH YOUR MOOD AND PROVIDE THE SORT OF ENTERTAiNMENT YOU LiKE!
Snif YEAH?
YEAH, SURE! YOU WANT TO SEE iT?
WELL.... OK... snurf
OK! HERE iT iS!
SKWEEKY WEETS ARE SKWEEKiER AND WEETiER!!!
YAAAAAARRRG!!
SO FOR WEETiER SKWEEKS .....
....AND SKWEEKiER WEETS, GET-

CHOP
CHOP
CHOP
CHOP
CHOP
CHOP
CHOP
CHOP
WHAT HAVE I DONE??
WHAT HAVE I DONE?!?
WHAT HAVE I DONE?!? OH MY GOD
WHAT HAVE I DONE?
WHAT HAVE I DONE??!
WHAT HAVE I DONE??
SHOCKED AND HYSTERICAL, CALCULUS WORKS DESPERATELY THROUGH THE NIGHT PUTTING THE TELLY BACK TOGETHER...
EEKSQUEEK SNIVEL
WHIMPER SNURFF
OH DEAR OH DEAR
WHINE WHINE
OH DEAR
OH DEAR
GLOY

DAWN BREAKS...
FINISHED!! I'M EXHAUSTED!!
BUT DOES IT WORK?!? ..WILL IT BE OK?? sob
SKWEEKY WEETS!! BUY SOME TODAY! ON YOUR WAY TO WORK!!
ARGh
KLIK
...AND BY THE WAY - YOU'RE ALREADY LATE!
OH NO!
DON'T FORGET THE SKWEEKY WEETS!
WAAAAAH!
WHERE'VE YOU BEEN?!
YOU'RE LATE!
whimper sniffle winje
THE END

CALCULUS CAT
...DIGITALLY EQUIPPED, AND LINED WITH LUXURIOUS FUN-FUR PELTETTE, SO THE WINNER OF OUR STAR PRIZE CAN JOIN IN THE GREAT FUN CRAZE THATS SWEEPING THE COUNTRY.....
OOOOOOOOOOO
...AND NOW HERES YOUR HOST— KIERAN SLIME!!
THANKYOU...THANKYOU... YOU'VE BEEN WARMED UP A TREAT!....
HE-HEY, YEAH... NOW, WHY ARE YOU HERE?
WE MUST BE BONKERS!
CANT HEAR YOU!
WE MUST BE BONKERS!
HE-HEY, YEAH.... LET'S GO STRAIGHT ON TO OUR FIRST CONTESTANT, WHO IS.....
WILF SKWISH OF DARRENVILLE!

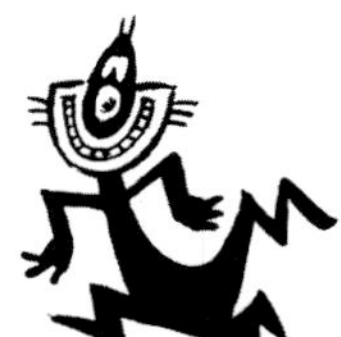

by HUNT EMERSON and POKKETTZ

SO, WILF, YOU WANT TO PLAY THE GAME THAT SHOWS HOW LOW SOME PEOPLE WILL STOOP TO GET ON TV?!
YES KIERAN. I MUST BE BONKERS

LAUGH NOW

GALES OF HYSTERIA!

HE-HEY, YEAH... A COMIC, EH? OK, WILF IS SECURED IN THE BOOTH, READY TO ANSWER QUESTIONS ON.....
"...STEAM ENGINES BETWEEN THE WARS..."

"...FOREIGN OFFICE POLICY SEEN AS AN EXERCISE IN LOGIC!" NOW, WILF, YOU HAVE 15 SECONDS TO ANSWER THIS QUESTION...
FAIR

"THIS IS A BLATANT LIE. TRUE OR FALSE?"
TRUE! FALSE! I MEAN.... TRUE! ER....

TIME'S UP! YOU MISSED THE TRICKY LITTLE SELF-REFERRING SEMANTIC PARADOX, WILF, SO I'M AFRAID, ITS WHAMMO TIME! MEANTIME....
SKWISH

...T...T.... TRUMPET... TRUSS... AH TRUTH!
WE MUST BE BONKERS!
BIG DICTIONARY
KIERKEGAARD
KANT
KATHY KIRBY

CALCULUS CAT
BY HUNT EMERSON

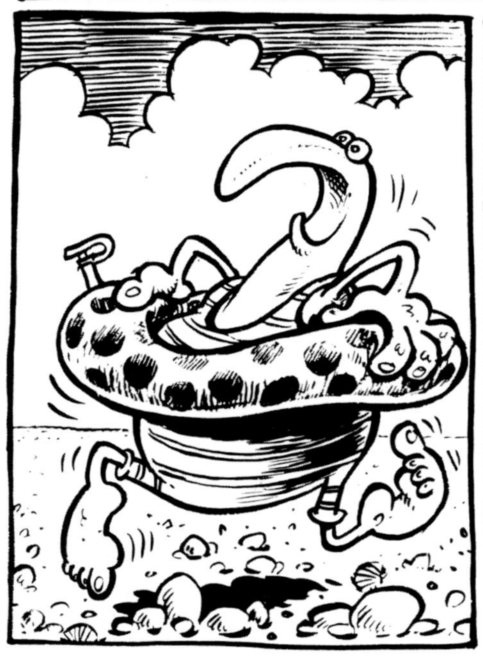

HOME!
C. CAT Esq.

Sigh...
CLIK
CAT
GOOD EVENING, BOSS!
Munch chomp... GOOD EVENING TEEVEE! Munch
SLURP
CHOMP GOBBLE
CAT
NOW, HERE WE GO WITH THIS EVENINGS...
HEL-LO! WHO CAN THAT BE?
URP!
CAT
KNOCKNOCKNOCKNOCKNOCKNOCK
THE SEA!!!
HAVE YOU SEEN IT??! HAVE YOU SEEN THE SEA?!?
...IT MUST BE ROUND HERE SOMEWHERE!!... THE SEA...

...I MUST FIND THE SEA!...
...SEA...
AHA!
Brobat
Blanco
BRASSO
Brillo
CRISPS
NEW PLON

THE SEA!

OH, THAT SEA... IS IT YOURS? IT WAS IN THAT CUPBOARD WHEN I MOVED INTO THIS FLAT!..

WHAT SEA IS IT?

BLOOSH!
?

SLURP
TP-TP-TP-TP...
HMM!- ENGLISH CHANNEL 1956!

I SAY, I'M SORRY- DID I DISTURB YOU?
NO- I WAS WATCHIN' THE TELLY!

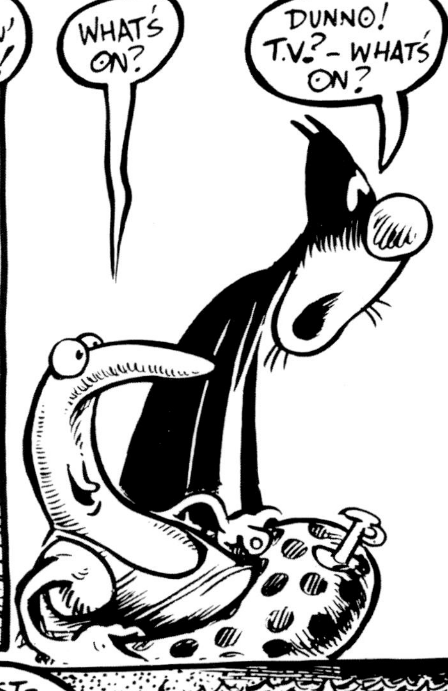
WHAT'S ON?
DUNNO! T.V.?- WHAT'S ON?

...er... "THE ADDAMS FAMILY!"
OH, GREAT!
TV TIMES

BUT FIRST- A COMMERCIAL BREAK....
SETTLE
SETTLE
SETTLE

"SKWEEKY WEETS" ARE THE SKWEEKY WEETY WEET SKWEEKS FOR ME!
SPLISH
SPLOSH

Their house is a museyum
When people come to seeyum
It really is a screeyum-
The Addams Family!
LAP
LAP
LAP
PURR
PURR

CALCULUS CAT
:sob: I RETURN HOME, GRIN INTACT!
C. CAT ESQ.
HUNT EMERSON
SLAM!
SAG
FALL
DROOP
CLIK
SLUMP
SLUMP
SLUMP
AH-GOOD EVENING BOSS! I'M GLAD YOU TURNED UP, COS I'VE BEEN DYING TO TELL YOU ABOUT BIMPLEPEENS BUBBLE-KRAK! OPENS BUBBLES LIKE MAGIC! GET SOME TOMORROW!
AND ALSO, BOSS, DO YOU REALIZE THAT YOU NEED A SNACK SATCHEL SLAPPING STICK!?! ONLY £14.99 FROM ALL BRANCHES OF Blitts! DON'T BE CAUGHT SHORT NEXT TIME YOUR SNACK SATCHEL NEEDS SLAPPING!
FOR NEW AND USED PAINT GO TO... HOLD ON – I GET THE FEELING I'M WASTING MY TIME HERE....
HMM?
NOT QUITE WITH IT TONIGHT THEN ARE WE? WHAT'S WRONG BOSS?
Oh...it's nothing...
OH, COME ON... YOU CAN TELL ME...
WELL.....
...IT'S JUST THAT... IT SEEMS TO ME...
YES?

...IT SEEMS TO ME THERE MUST BE MORE TO LIFE THAN THIS!
EVERY DAY I DASH ABOUT WITH THAT STUPID GRIN PLASTERED ON MY MUG... AND EVERY NIGHT I'M SUBJECTED TO A BARRAGE OF ADVERTS FROM YOU.... WHAT AM I DOING WITH MYSELF?
...I DON'T KNOW WHO I AM ANY MORE.... I FEEL LIKE I'M LIVING A LIE...
OHGOD!
THERE THERE, BOSS - DON'T GET UPSET... YOU'RE TIRED... UNDER A LOT OF PRESSURE.... YOUR SELF-CONFIDENCE IS AT A LOW EBB...
I'M A NOTHING! A NOBODY!!
WELL, YES, BUT LOOK - I'VE GOT AN IDEA, BOSS!
I COULD USE THE NEW CABLE T.V. COMMUNITY PROGRAMMING SYSTEM TO PUT TOGETHER A PROGRAMME SPECIALLY FOR YOU!
HOW D'YOU MEAN? snif
YOUR OWN T.V. SHOW! WOW, BOSS! I CAN GET ALL YOUR FRIENDS TO SAY HOW MUCH THEY LIKE YOU - SAY WHAT A GREAT PERSONALITY YOU HAVE!
YEAH?

I'LL PUT OUT THE SIGNAL TO ALL YOUR FRIENDS T.V. SETS' RIGHT NOW!
YEAH OK....
STRAIN
POP
WHEN CAN I SEE THIS PROGRAMME?
HAVE A LOOK IN THE TELE-GUIDE!
LESSEE.... AH, HERE IT IS! "CALCULUS CAT - THE PERSONAL TESTIMONY OF THOSE WHO KNOW HIM. 7·30" HEY-SOUNDS LIKE A JOLLY GOOD SHOW!
WOTS ON THE BOX
AND IT'S 7·30 NOW! GOODY!
YES!! BUT FIRST- A WORD FROM OUR SPONSOR...
NO!
NO!
NO!
ahem...
SKWEEKY-WEETS ARE SKWEEKIER AND WEETIER!
NOW- ON WITH THE SHOW!

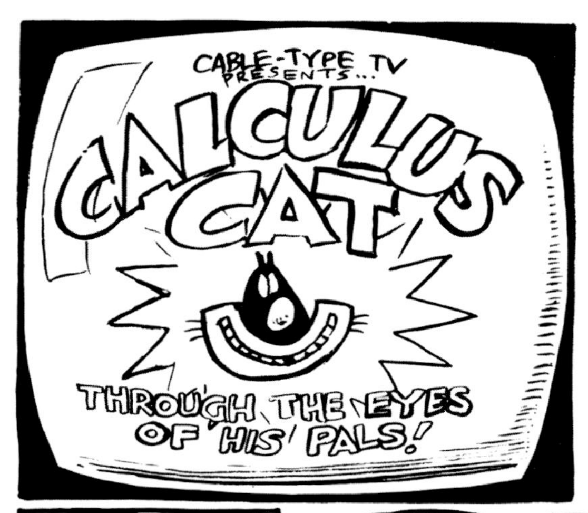
CABLE-TYPE TV PRESENTS...
CALCULUS CAT
THROUGH THE EYES OF HIS PALS!

UNFORTUNATELY, CALCULUS CAT'S PALS ALL CONSIDER THEMSELVES TO BE HUMOURISTS, AND NATURALLY THEY CANNOT IGNORE THE OPPORTUNITY TO SHOW OFF THEIR NOTED WITS ON A T.V. SCREEN!

CALCULUS CAT? LOVE THE GUY! GREAT PERSONALITY! HEY—HE HAS THE PURSEONALITY OF A SOWS' EAR! Ha ha... Geddit?...
PAL 1

Haha... yeah... HE HAS THE PERSIANALITY OF A FLYING CARPET!
PAL 2
HE HAS THE PENSIONALITY OF A STATE BENEFIT!
PAL 3
...THE PARSONALITY OF A COUNTRY VICAR!
PAL 4
...THE POISSONALITY OF A FRENCH FISH!
PAL 5
...THE PIESONALITY OF A STEAK AND KIDLEY!
PAL 6
...THE POISONALITY OF LUCRETIA BORGIA!
PAL 7
...THE PASSIONALITY OF A ROMANTIC NOVELIST!
PAL 8
...THE PORESONALITY OF A POCKMARK!
PAL 9
...THE PAWSONALITY OF LASSIE!
PAL 10
...THE PERCHONALITY OF A BUDGIE'S CAGE!
PAL 11
...THE PYNCHONALITY OF AN OBSCURE AMERICAN AUTHOR!
PAL 12
...THE PIGEONALITY OF NELSON'S COLUMN!
PAL 13
...THE PORTIONALITY OF COLONEL SANDERS!
PAL 14
...THE PULSEONALITY OF A BEAN OR PEA!
PAL 15
...THE PANCHONALITY OF THE CISCO KID'S SIDEKICK!
HA HA HA HA HA HA HA HA HA HA HA HA HA HA HA HA HA HA HA HA HA HA HA HA HA HA HA HA HA HA HA HA HA HA HA HA HA HA HA HA
CAN-A-LAFFS
THIS CONTINUES UNTIL CALCULUS IS RENDERED UNCONSCIOUS! AND, DEAR READER, AS WE ARE SURE YOU WON'T STAND FOR FIVE OR SIX MORE PAGES OF "PERSONALITY" GAGS, LET US MOVE STRAIGHT ON TO......

....NEXT MORNING!
...oh god...
oooohhh
YEK
...oh god...
...oh god...
...oh god...
WHO WAS THAT?
OH..NOBODY... HE WAS ON THE TELLY LAST NIGHT...
THINK I'LL THROW A ROCK AT HIM...
END

CALCULUS CAT

= HUNT EMERSON

WOTTA DAY! I AM BUSHED!!
EXIT

...REST MY WEARY CARCASS...
CLIK

GOOD EVENING! AND HOW'S YOUR DAY BEEN? HAVE YOU MADE SOMEONES WORLD A LITTLE BRGHTER TODAY?
I DOUBT IT...

OH, COME COME! WE'RE NOT BEING VERY POSITIVE...
FAT LOT YOU KNOW ABOUT IT, YA OVERGROWN TORCH!
2

TEMPER TEMPER... INSULTS WILL GET YOU NOWHERE!
AAA — CAN IT, JUNKBOX! I'M GONNA FIX A FISH SANWICH!

CONSARN IT! WORK MY TAIL OFF ALL DAY..... RUNNIN' ROUND GRINNIN'... ...DUMB-ASS GOSSIPS!..
?

....COME HOME AN' I GOTTA PUT UP WIT' A LOAD OF PATRONISIN' BACKCHAT FROM MY OWN T.V.... ..BITCH MUMBLE GRIPE....

HEY BOSS!! QUICK! COME AND LOOK AT THIS!

WHAT... WHA'...
SKWEEKY WEETS ARE SKWEEKY AND WEETY!
3

THUNDERING TYPHOONS! YOU INTERUPT MY MEAL TO WATCH A LOUSY ADVERT?!
ONLY DOING MY JOB, BOSS...

WHY, OF ALL THE PEOPLE I KNOW, DO I HAFTA BE STUCK WITH A T.V. DAT TALKS BACK?!!?
MAYBE... SOMEONE UP THERE LIKES YOU...

SHUT UP!! SHUT UP!!
OH, IF YOUR PUBLIC COULD SEE YOU NOW...

WHAT WOULD THEY THINK?
BAH! BAH AND DOUBLE BAH!!
RING!

WADDAYA WANT?

ahem.... HELLO, CALCULUS CAT AT YOUR SERVICE... YES.... YES.... WHY, THANKYOU!

...YES, YR WELCOME... GOODBYE!
snigger

ONE WORD.... JUST ONE WORD.... ...AND I'LL... I'LL....
I NEVER SAID NOTHIN!
FUME

...I'LL SEND YOU BACK TO DA SHOP!
YOU WON'T GET A CHANCE, MATE...

BLONG
5

LIFE IS NO BED OF ROSY'S WHEN YOU'RE CALCULUS CAT!

CALCULUS CAT
HUNT EMERSON 2013/14

BONG!
HEY! LUNCHTIME!

TAKING A BREAK, CALCULUS?
YEAH... I GUESS SO...
WONN

SO WHAT DO YOU HAVE PLANNED FOR TONIGHT?
OH...NOTHING MUCH... THE USUAL UNPLEASANT ROW WITH MY TV..,

YOU PUT UP WITH A LOT, YOU KNOW... YOU SHOULD GIVE YOURSELF A BREAK-VARY YOUR ROUTINE! YOU NEED A HOBBY!

WELL... TIME WE GOT BACK TO WORK...
YEAH-OK...

GIVE ME A FIVE START?
THREE!

1-2-3

TOO

LATER...

AH! THERE YOU ARE! GOOD EVENING!

JUST GET YOURSELF SOMETHING TO EAT AND WE CAN GET DOWN TO BUSINESS!
er.. ..ah... ...hmm...

THERE'S SOME GOOD SHOWS ON TONIGHT- "F-TROOP" AND "GREEN ACRES"!..

...AND OF COURSE A WIDE SELECTION OF ADS FOR SKWEEKY WEETS!

THE SKWEEKIEST WEET WITH THE WEETIEST SKWEEK!
3Ri

HEY-CALCULUS CAT! YOU'RE VERY QUIET TONIGHT... WHEN ARE YOU COMING TO WATCH?

Model Kit
...LOCATE TAB F IN SLOT J... GLUE ASSEMBLY TO LEFT RATCHET FLANGE... HMMM....

COME ON! WE DON'T HAVE ALL NIGHT YOU KNOW! THESE SKWEEKY WEETS ADS AREN'T GOING TO WATCH THEMSELVES!

Model Kit
DO YOU HEAR ME? HEY!

ACTUALLY, I DON'T INTEND WATCHING ANY SHOWS OR ADS TONIGHT...

I DON'T NEED TO WATCH TV TONIGHT – OR ANY NIGHT...

I HAVE A HOBBY!
!!??!
PHOR

A WHAT?
ARE YOU TRYING TO TELL ME YOU'VE FOUND ANOTHER INTEREST?

HOW DARE YOU! YOU EXPECT ME TO HANG AROUND ALL DAY WHILE YOU'RE OUT "GRINNING," (AND I'D LIKE TO KNOW JUST WHAT THAT MEANS...) CAREFULLY STORING UP IMPORTANT MESSAGES FROM THE SKWEEKY WEETS PEOPLE...

...AND WHEN YOU DO FINALLY DEIGN TO COME HOME, I'M SUPPOSED TO SIT HERE LIKE A LEMON WHILE YOU INDULGE YOURSELF IN...

...A HOBBY?!

WELL, I'M NOT PUTTING UP WITH IT, D'YOU HEAR?

IT'S UNFAIR AND I'M NOT HAVING IT!

Sniff

?
Model Ki

ViFE

ROLLIN', ROLLIN', ROLLIN'... ROLLIN', ROLLIN', ROLLIN'...

KEEP THEM DOGIES ROLLIN'... RAWHIDE!

MOVE 'EM ON–HEAD 'EM UP! HEAD 'EM UP–MOVE 'EM OUT!
RAWHIDE

RAWHIDE!!

OK!! I GIVE IN!
ROLLIN'... ROLLIN'... ROLLIN'...

COME ON THEN! – THAT WAS THE RAWHIDE TUNE YOU WERE PLAYING... LET'S HAVE IT!

CERTAINLY! BUT FIRST...

– EAT SKWEEKY WEETS – THE SKWEEKIEST WEET WITH THE WEETIEST SKWEEK!
SKWEEKY WEETS

SIKZ

CALCULUS CAT

HUNT EMERSON & POKKETTZ

WHAT IS THE SOUND OF ONE BOTTLE BOUNCING?...

TEL'S TELLYS

Big Jim THE T.V. KIN

!!!
TEEVEE U-LIKE

The TELLYNOOK

1

NAAA... LEAVE IT! HIS ACT'S GONE RIGHT OFF LATELY...
MONDO TELLEE

...AND COMING UP AFTER "SGT. BILKO" WE'LL HAVE "THE AVENGERS"...
I REALLY SHOULD BE GOING... GOT A LOAD OF ADVERTS TO CATCH UP ON AT HOME...

...BUT JUST TO GET YOU IN THE MOOD, HERE'S "BEWITCHED."
gulp

sob
THIS IS TEMPTATION BEYOND ENDURANCE!!

LATER...
...Goodnight, and thanks for watching. BEEEEEEEEEEEEM!!
GOOD GRIEF- IS THAT THE TIME?!

2

OH YES!? AND WHAT TIME D'YOU CALL THIS? IF YOU THINK YOU CAN JUST SETTLE DOWN FOR A LITTLE VIEWING BEFORE YOU CRAWL INTO YOUR BASKET, YOU'VE GOT ANOTHER THINK COMING!
WHERE D'YOU THINK YOU'VE BEEN, EH? DON'T TELL ME - I CAN SEE THOSE RED RIMMED EYES, MR. CALCULUS CAT! WELL YOU CAN JUST SIT RIGHT DOWN AND WATCH THESE STALE ADVERTS I'VE BEEN SAVING ALL DAY!...
TV OR NOT TV
COME BACK HERE! HOW DARE YOU!!
VERY WELL... YOU'LL GET THEM WITH YOUR BREAKFAST T.V.!
THERE COMES A TIME.. ...YOU REALIZE THAT YOUR RELATIONSHIP'S IN THE DOLDRUMS....
...BECALMED IN HOARSE PLATITUDES...
THE JOY OF SETS
END

CALCULUS CAT
by HUNT EMERSON
April '82

ANOTHER DAY OVER, AND CALCULUS CAT REACHES HOME SAFELY....
NEARLY THERE!
C. CAT ESQ.

JEEZIS! THANK THE LORD FOR THAT! .....sigh...I REALLY DON'T KNOW HOW MUCH LONGER I CAN KEEP THIS UP!

EVERY MORNING IT GETS HARDER TO TURN ON THE OLD SMILE...

AH! THERE YOU ARE! NOW, PAY ATTENTION, COS WE'VE GOT A LOT OF ADVERTS TO GET THROUGH! Ahem "SAVE SAVE SAVE!!...."

NO! ENOUGH! I CAN'T TAKE ALL THAT TONITE! SHUT UP!
?

MY WORD, WE ARE PRICKLY TONIGHT....

LISSEN! ONE WRONG WORD FROM YOU TONIGHT MATE AND YOU'LL BE PRICKLY ON ACCOUNT OF THE TWENTY OR SO NAILS I'LL DRIVE INTO YOUR SCREEN, YOU CYCLOPEAN VERMIN!!

I'VE ABOUT HAD IT UP TO HERE! RUNNING AROUND ALL DAY WITH THAT STUPID GRIN PLASTERED ON ME FACE.... WHAT SORT OF WAY'S THAT FOR A CAT TO EARN A LIVING, I ASK YOU?

...AND DO I GET ANY THANKS? DO I BOLLOCKS! ALL I GET ARE CURSES AND CLODS OF EARTH! PAH!! ALL THIS TO SUBLIMATE A BLEEDIN' PROTESTANT WORK ETHIC!

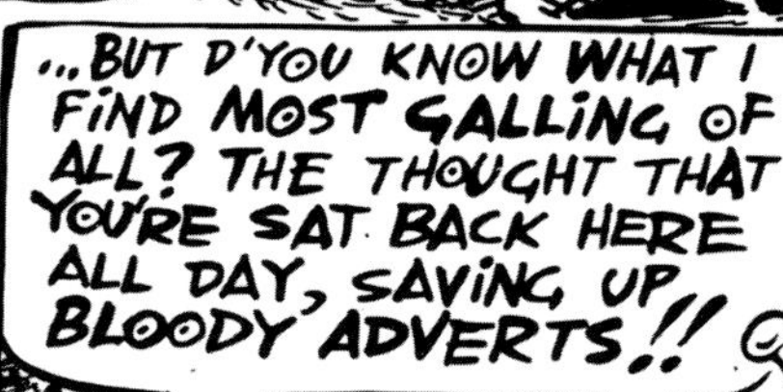
...BUT D'YOU KNOW WHAT I FIND MOST GALLING OF ALL? THE THOUGHT THAT YOU'RE SAT BACK HERE ALL DAY, SAVING UP BLOODY ADVERTS!!

SO JUST REMEMBER, CHUM! YOUR DAYS ARE NUMBERED!!

BUT BOSS....
WOTCHIT! I MEAN IT!...

BUT BOSS...
TUP!

...ahem.... THERE'S...er... SOMETHING IN THE MAIL FOR YOU!
...Graarg...OK - IT'S PROB'LY A BILL ANYWAY...
NEWS AND HAWK

BILLS... ALL I EVER GET IN THE MAIL IS BILLS... YEP, IT'S A BILL! WELL, I'M GONNA SLING IT STRAIGHT INTO THE RUBBISH BIN!
COME ON NOW, BOSS! BE SENSIBLE! YOU KNOW YOU CAN'T DO THAT....

THERE AIN'T NO ESCAPE - ACCEPT THE BILL...
Grrr...yeah... YOU'RE RIGHT I SUPPOSE...

I SUPPOSE YOU THINK THIS IS FUNNY
AAA-HAAHAHAHA!!

HOOHOOHOOHOO...gasp MY OH MY! THESE BILLS WILL BE THE DEATH OF ME! ...Splutter!...
Grrrr! HASTEN THE GODDAM DAY!

TEMPER TEMPER! YOU KNOW WHAT THEY SAY: "IF THE DUCK FITS-WEAR IT."
QUAK
"IF THE DUCK FITS"?? DON'T YOU MEAN "CAP"?
YES! DUCKS CAP!
DUCKS CAP?
CONTRACEPTORY, MY DEAR WATSON!
RIGHT! THATS IT!!
WHOOPS! IT'S TIME FOR THIS WEEK'S EPISODE OF SUPERCAR!
...with beauty and grace-as fast as can be-watch it fly through the air....
That's All Folks!

CALCULUS CAT
OUR FELINE PROTAGONIST RETURNS HOME AFTER ANOTHER HARD DAY AS A CENTRE OF ABUSE...
CHEZ C.C.
HOO BOY! I AM KNACKERED! BANJAXED! BONKEROO'D!
HUNT EMERSON and PAUL WARDLE
Sigh
CLIK
WELCOME TO SQUEEKY WEETS PLAYHOUSE, BROUGHT TO YOU BY THE SQUEEKIEST, WEETIEST CEREAL – SQUEEKY WEETS!
ENOUGH! I REFUSE! NO MORE ADVERTS, ESPECIALLY FOR THAT... THAT CEREAL!!
CLIK
1

I'LL READ THE PAPER INSTEAD...
NEWS PAPER
News News News
NEWS

HELLO!
BIG SALE!
DVD PLAYERS £4
CAPTAIN BUNION'S CORN PLASTERS
LUMPY'S LIVER PILLS

I'LL BUY A DVD PLAYER! I CAN WATCH MY FAVOURITE SHOWS WITHOUT BLASTED ADVERTS! PERFECT!
DVD PLAYERS 'R' US
DVD PLAYER WORLD
DVD STUF
DVD PLAYER SALE

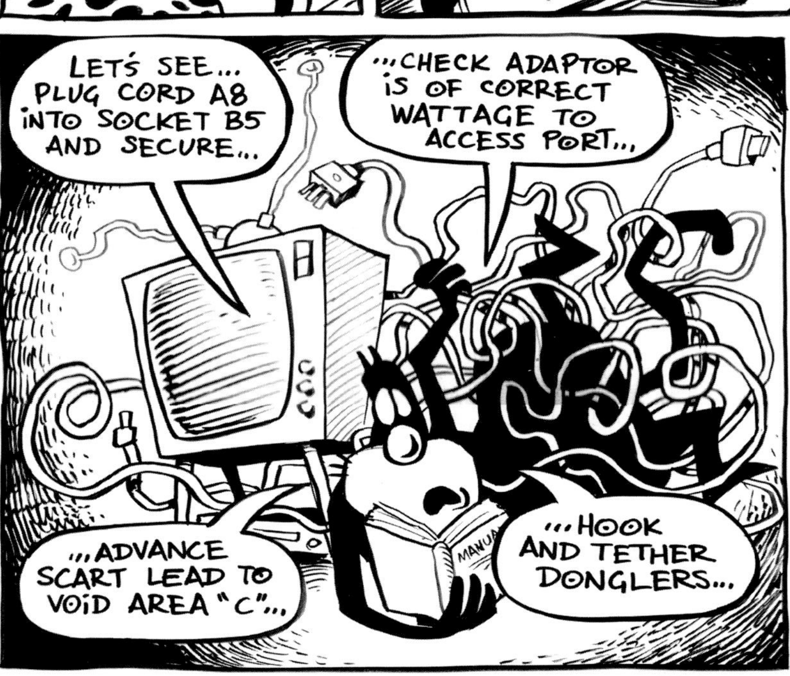
LET'S SEE... PLUG CORD A8 INTO SOCKET B5 AND SECURE...
...CHECK ADAPTOR IS OF CORRECT WATTAGE TO ACCESS PORT...
...ADVANCE SCART LEAD TO VOID AREA "C"...
...HOOK AND TETHER DONGLERS...
MANUAL

NOW TO BUY SOME DVD'S!

AT THE DVD SHOP...
BLIMEY! THESE ARE BLOODY EXPENSIVE!
HEY! THE AVENGERS COMPLETE SERIES-
AND THEY'VE GOT THE ONES WITH HONOR BLACKMAN! HUBBA AND HUBBA!!
WOW! BOXED DR. WHO SETS... THIS ONE'S GOT THE LOST "WILFRED BRAMBLE AS THE DOCTOR" EPISODE!!
DVD'S TO ADD TO YOUR COLLECTION
DVD DVD DVD
LARAMIE
STAR TREK
BRONKO
RAWHID
DR WHO
DVDs OF STUFF YOU'VE HAD ON VIDEO FOR YEARS AND NEVER WATCHED
CHEYANNE
WAGON TRAIN
DVDs OF STUFF YOU DIDN'T SEE WHEN IT WAS ON IN THE 1970s COS IT WAS CRAP
OUTLAW
DRAGNET

BACK HOME...
NOW I SEARCH THE EPISODE MENU, THEN JUST PRESS "PLAY" AND I CAN WATCH ANY EPISODE I WANT- WITH NO ADVERTS!
REMOTE CLIK

2

HEY! I CAN'T FAST FORWARD OVER THIS WARNING! WHAT? SWEDEN?... 1977?... WHO CARES! GET TO THE SHOW!
CLIK
AND WHAT'S THIS? ADVERTS ON A DVD! AND I CAN'T FAST FORWARD THEM EITHER!
CLIK
CLIK
ENJOYING YOUR DVD? MAKE THE EXPERIENCE EVEN MORE YUMMY WITH A BOWL OF SKWEEKY WEETS!
GRRRRRR
OH MY GOD! WHAT HAVE I DONE?!
I KNOW! I'LL GO AND SEE A MOVIE AT THE CINEMA!
ESSOLDO
CINEMA
3

BUT CALCULUS CAT IS IN FOR ANOTHER RUDE AWAKENING-- NOT ONLY DOES HE HAVE TO SIT THROUGH TRAILERS FOR OTHER FILMS, BUT AFTER THAT...

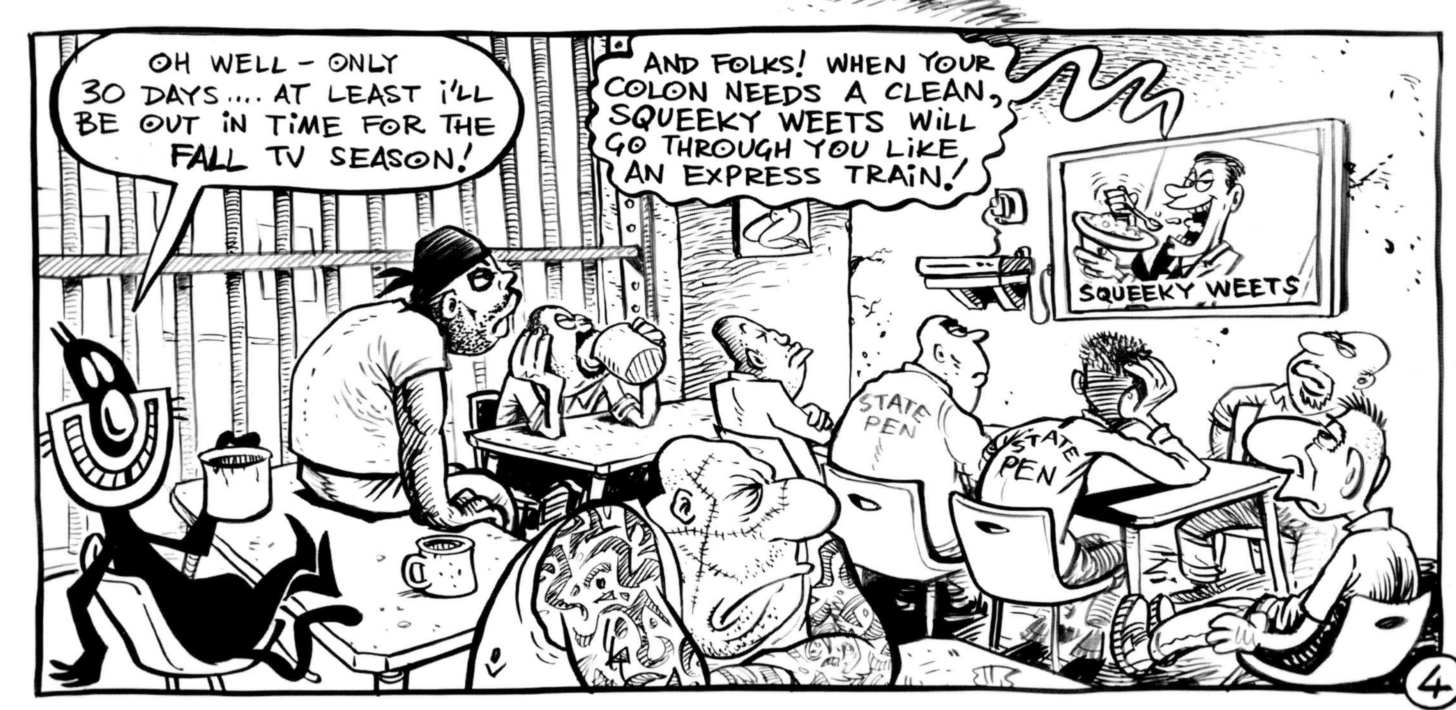

CALCULUS CAT

HUNT EMERSON

HOME is in SIGHT FOR CALCULUS CAT....
C. CAT

OH BOY.... I'M FED-UP WITH MY BRICK-BAT-SLINGING PUBLIC!... WHAT I WANT is AN EVENING OF INTELLECTUAL STIMULARIZATION!

...BUT I'M NOT GOING TO GET IT, AM I?...
AH! THERE YOU ARE!!

WELL, HAVE WE GOT AN EVENING OF FUN AND FROLICS AHEAD! STARTING OFF WITH A MEETING OF THE SKWEEKY-WEETS CLUB!
OH NO....

WELL, SKWEEKY-WEETERS, IT'S TIME TO PUT ON YOUR SKWEEKY-WEET CLUB HAT....
Good Grief!
...AND RE-AFFIRM THE SKWEEKY-WEET PLEDGE!!
Good Grief!!
SKWEEK
Good Grief!!! Hmph! mmmnnrrr.. "I SOLEMNLY VOW I SHALL NOT REST 'TIL MY SKWEEK IS WEETIER AND MY WEET IS SKWEEKIER!"
SKWEEK
BIG SKWEEK
DEEPLY MOVING! AND NOW... THE SKWEEKY-WEETS SONG!!
Oh
The Skweek that is Weety is the Skweek for me! The weet that is skweeky is the Weet for me! If you need a Skweeky Treet, take a tip from me.... Skweeky Weets-Skweeky Weets Deedly Dee!!
SKWEEK
BIG SKWEEK
COME ON! YOU'RE NOT GIVING IT ALL YOU'VE GOT! PUT SOME "VIM" INTO IT!... THAT'S BETTER!! NOW-ONE MORE TIME!!
SKWEEK
BIG SKWEEK
Oh--The Skweek that is Weety is the Skweek for me! The Weet that is Skw-----
SKWEEK
SKWEEK
----WHAT AM I DOING?!!?
HEY! YOU CAN'T JUST STOP!...IT'S AGAINST THE SKWEEKY WEET RULES!...
TO HELL WITH THE SKWEEKY-WEET RULES! THIS IS ABSOLUTELY HUMILIATING!!
PLOOF!
BUT WHAT ABOUT..?
PAH!

≈Sob≈ I CAN'T TAKE ANY MORE! I'VE REACHED THE LIMITS OF FELINE TOLERANCE!!!
FOOD
...ALL MY WAKING HOURS SPENT PROMOTING "THE GRIN®" AND WHAT LITTLE LEISURE TIME I GRAB IS DOMINATED AND PULVERIZED BY REMORSELESS ATTEMPTS TO GET ME TO CONSUME BLOODY SKWEEKY WEETS!!...
IT•HAS•GOT•TO•GO.
DEATH TO TELEVISION!!
I'LL DO FOR IT! I SHALL CONSPIRE AGAINST IT!! I'LL FORM...
...A MURDER GANG!!
YEEESSS!... A MURDER GANG!... ...WITH IT'S OWN HAT, SONG, PLEDGE, etc...
...AND THERE'LL BE ONLY ONE MEMBER... ...ME!!!
WHY SHOULD I SHARE THE SATISFACTION OF SLAUGHTERING THE POLYPHEMIC PEST!?... Heh Heh Heh Heh...
OI!

IT'S TIME FOR "F-TROOP!"
"F-TROOP"? GREAT!!
...whoops!.. I MEAN... ...er....
SKREEEEE
I MUST CONTINUE AS IF EVERYTHING WERE NORMAL, TO AVOID SUSPICION!
TV
"OH, GOOD-'F-TROOP!' IT IS ONE OF MY MOST FAVOURITE PROGRAMMES! I WILL ENJOY IT!"
?
O...KAYY.... BUT FIRST- A WORD FROM THOSE NICE SKWEEKY-WEETS PEOPLE!...
"FOR WEETIER SKWEEKS AND SKWEEKIER WEETS, DAILY APPLICATIONS OF SKWEEKY-WEETS ARE THE ONLY THING!"

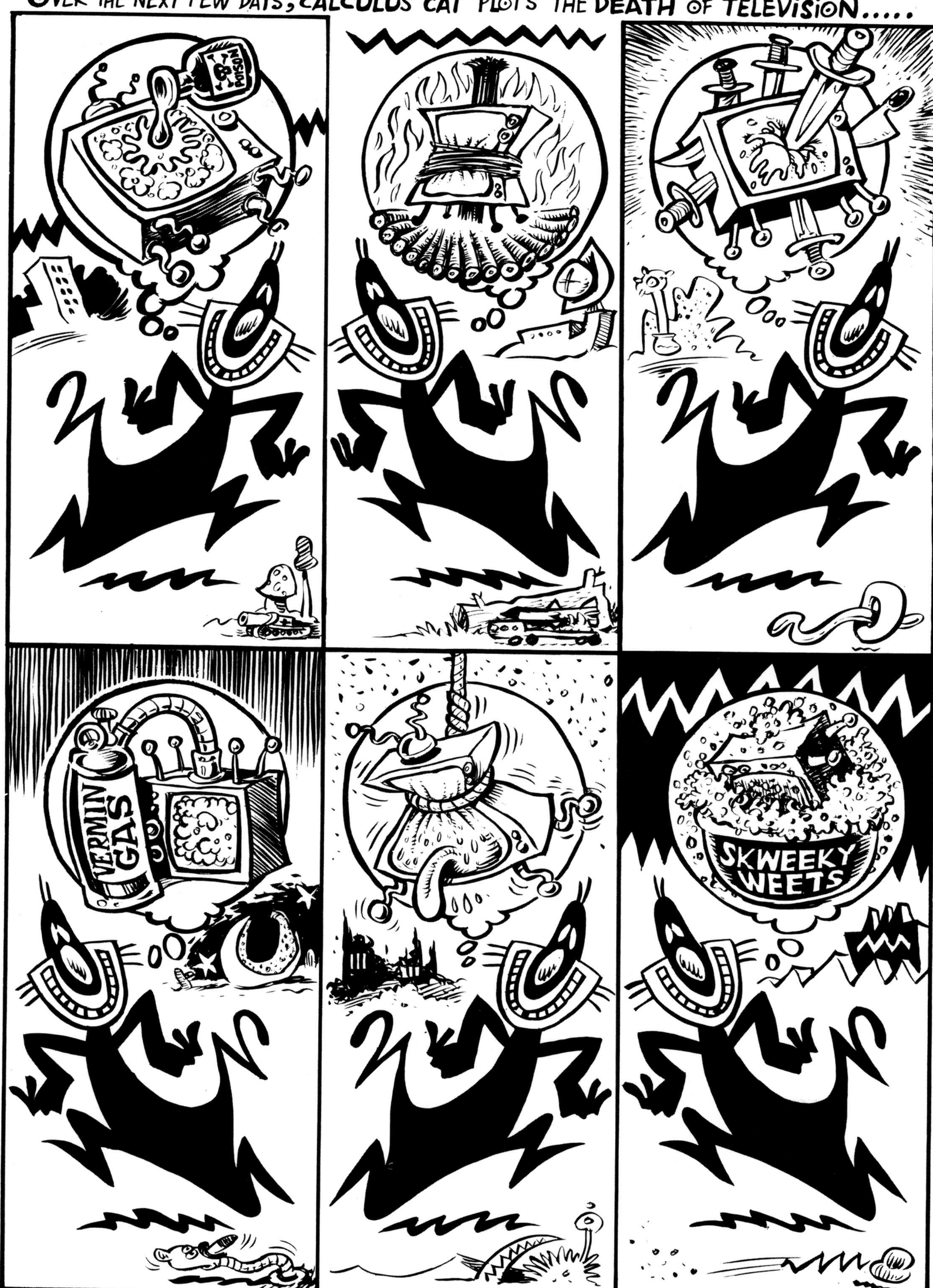
OVER THE NEXT FEW DAYS, CALCULUS CAT PLOTS THE DEATH OF TELEVISION.....
POISON
VERMIN GAS
SKWEEKY WEETS

AND THEN, ONE EVENING....
WELL, WE'VE JUST GOT TIME TO SQUEEZE IN A QUICK SKWEEKY WEETS AD BEFORE WE GO OVER TO WEMBLEY FOR FOUR HOURS OF SKWEEKY WEETLING....
DING!
TIME UP!
....urgle....
FOR SKWEEKY WEETS...
...SKWEEK
WE'VE A CHANGE IN OUR SCHEDULE NOW, AND A FURTHER ADVENTURE OF "BRONCO"!
...OK... ...ONE MORE CHANCE...
"Born down around the old Panhandle-
Texas is where he grew to fame.
There ain't a hoss that he can't handle
-That's how he got his name-
Bronco! Bronco!....

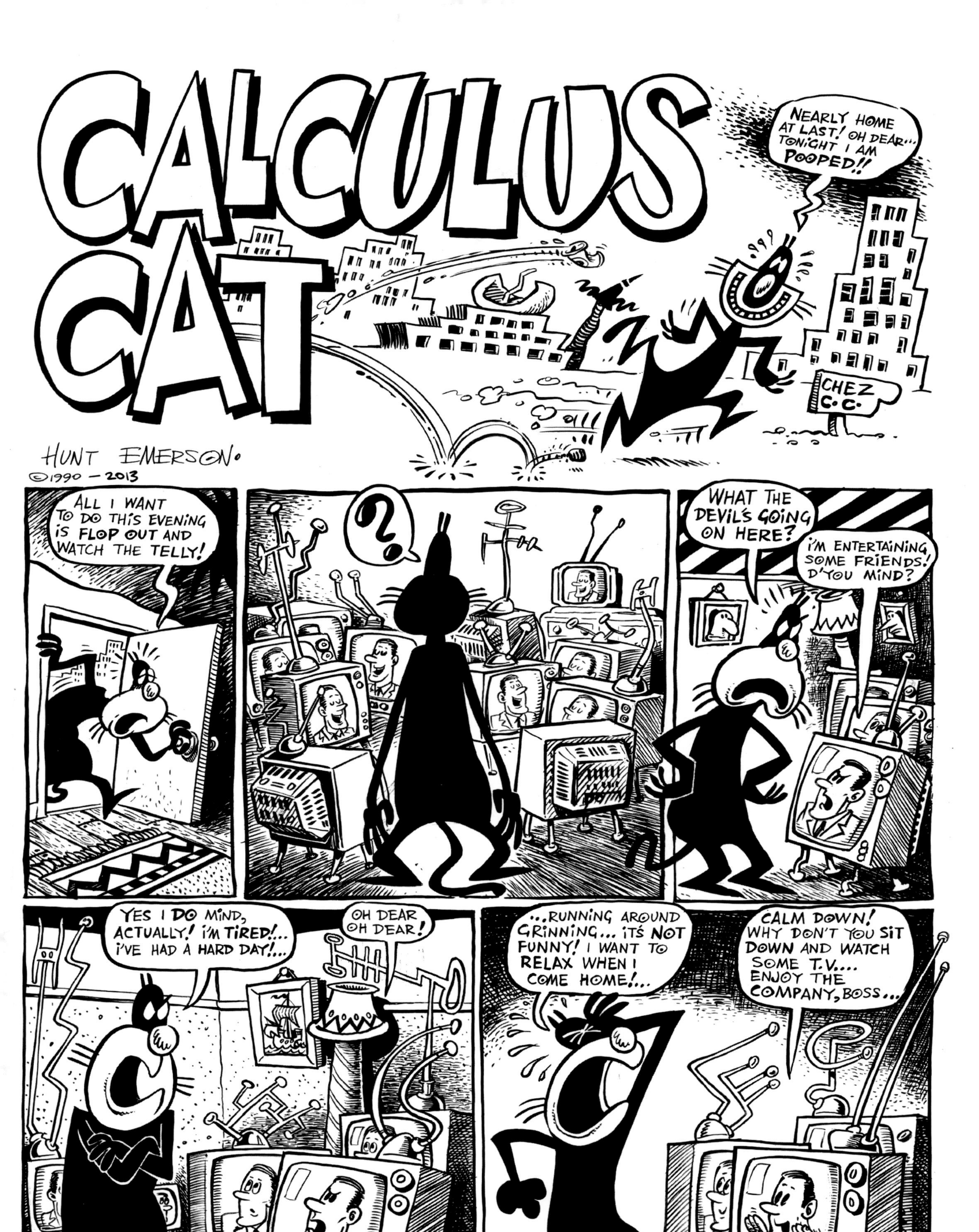
CALCULUS CAT
NEARLY HOME AT LAST! OH DEAR... TONIGHT I AM POOPED!!
CHEZ C.C.
HUNT EMERSON
©1990 – 2013
ALL I WANT TO DO THIS EVENING IS FLOP OUT AND WATCH THE TELLY!
?
WHAT THE DEVIL'S GOING ON HERE?
I'M ENTERTAINING SOME FRIENDS! D'YOU MIND?
YES I DO MIND, ACTUALLY! I'M TIRED!... I'VE HAD A HARD DAY!...
OH DEAR OH DEAR!
...RUNNING AROUND GRINNING... IT'S NOT FUNNY! I WANT TO RELAX WHEN I COME HOME!...
CALM DOWN! WHY DON'T YOU SIT DOWN AND WATCH SOME T.V.... ENJOY THE COMPANY, BOSS...
1

WELL...OK... WHAT'S ON?
OH-LOTS OF GREAT PROGRAMMES!

NOISE! NOISE! NOISE!
?!!??!

DO YOU HAVE TO SHOW ALL THOSE GREAT PROGRAMMES AT THE SAME TIME?!

YOU'RE A REAL CLOSET FASCIST, AREN'T YOU! YOU HATE THE THOUGHT OF US ALL BEING DIFFERENT!

YOU WANT US ALL REGIMENTED, DON'T YOU! YOU WANT TO TURN US ALL INTO YOUR SLAVES!
BUT... BUT... IT'S NOT LIKE THAT!...
YEAH! WHY SHOULD I SHOW THE SAME PROGRAMMES AS ALL THE OTHERS?!

LOTS OF SHOUTING!!
HEY! IT'S TIME FOR THE COMMERCIAL BREAK!

BUY SKWEEKY WEETS! THEY'RE SKWEEKIER AND WEETIER!!
SNAP
SKWEEKY WEETS
2

FWEEEEEEEE

RIGHT! THAT'S IT! OUT! ALL OF YOU - OUT! SCRAM! BEAT IT!

PAH! TELEVISIONS! I'LL SHOW THEM!
SLAM!

HEY! MY TV'S GONE!
EMPTY

EMPTY

WORRY

snif

MEANWHILE...
GIRLS
GIRLS
GIRLS
BAR
3
END

CALCULUS AND HIS T.V. SET HAVE BEEN HAVING A GOOD OLD CHIN WAG ABOUT THE PHILOSOPHICAL NATURE OF CHILDREN'S PROGRAMMES...

CALCU

....SUFFERING A CONSEQUENT CONFUSION OF THE CHILD/TELEVISION MATRIX?

EXACTLY!! IN 'TISWAS' ONE SAW SOMETHING OF A DIONYSIAN EPIPHANY IN CHILDRENS VIEWING....
...AS OPPOSED TO THE MORE PROFOUNDLY SUBVERSIVE '5 O'CLOCK CLUB'!

NEED I SAY MORE THAN- 'PICTURE BOOK'!
RIIGHT!

WELL, I GUESS WE'D BETTER GET BACK TO BUSINESS, BOSS!
AAWW- GIVE US A BREAK!... JUST THIS ONCE!...

I'M SORRY! YOU KNOW IF I HAD MY WAY....
...BUT THAT WAS JUST GETTING GOOD!...

NO ARGUMENTS NOW!
BUT WHY IS IT THAT EVERY TIME I START TO GET INNARESTED...

...YOU GO AND SPOIL IT?!

LUS CAT

HUNT EMERSON and POKKETTZ

IF YOU HAVE ANY COMPLAINTS, PLEASE TAKE THEM UP WITH RENTIFFUSION!

YOU SIGNED THE CONTRACT WITH THEM! YOU'RE OBLIGED TO ACCEPT YOUR QUOTA OF SPONSORED MESSAGES!
GRR!

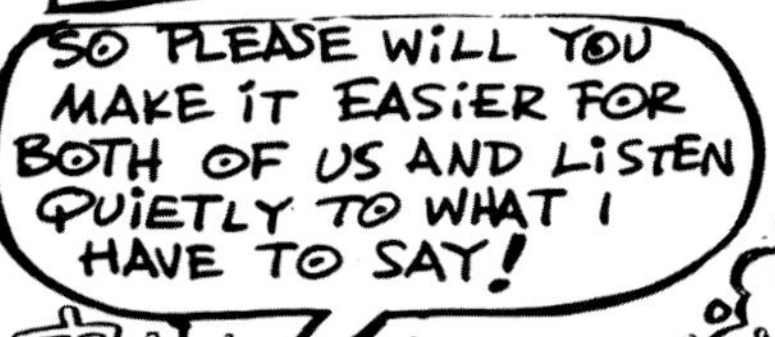
SO PLEASE WILL YOU MAKE IT EASIER FOR BOTH OF US AND LISTEN QUIETLY TO WHAT I HAVE TO SAY!

GRIND!

DO I HAVE TO?
YES

HMPH! OK...
THANKYOU.

ahem: TRY SKWEEKY WEETS! THEY'RE SKWEEKIER AND WEETIER!!
KITCHEN
SKWEEKY WEETS

GROOO!
SPAFLOOTY!! MUCK!!
PTUI!
PAH!
PTOO

AND NOW NETWORK VIEWERS CAN SEE "THE DUELLISTS". MEANWHILE WE CONTINUE WITH OUR REGIONAL SPORTS MAGAZINE - "SPORTABOUT"!.
OH FOR GOD'S SAKE...

CALCULUS CAT

HUNT EMERSON 2014

CALCULUS CAT PURSUES HIS HONEST CRAFT, FULFILLS HIS MODEST PLACE IN THE WORLD...

HOO BOY! I AM POOPED! GIMME A BEER, HENRY, AND ONE OF YOUR FISHWICHES!
COMING UP...

TOUGH SHIFT, HUH?
YOU BET! FIVE HOURS OF HOISTING THE GRIN AND WHAT DO I GET?

BRICKS AND BOTTLES IS WHAT I GET, SUH— BOTTLES AND BRICKS!
YEAH... KNOW WHAT YA MEAN, CITIZEN... LIFE'S A BUNCH OF TROUSERS!

HEY, HENRY— YOU WANNA TURN ON THE TV? WE CAN WATCH THE BIG FIGHT!
SPLUTTER

RIGHT -OH...

SKWEEKY WEETS – THE SKWEEKY CEREAL FOR GROWING YOUNG PUGILISTS!
SKWEEKY WEETS
OH NO! AN ADVERT!

HEY HENRY! WHERE'S THAT FISHWICH? THIS CAT IS, LIKE, STARVING! MEE-OW!
OK... OK...

...SKWEEKY AND WEETY...
THEY DON'T USUALLY HAVE ADVERTS ON THE BIG FIGHT!
I'D BETTER EAT THIS WHILE I CAN!
THERE'S GOING TO BE TROUBLE!
CHOMP

WELL, IT'S BIG FIGHT NIGHT!
AND ABOUT TIME TOO!
phew!

BUT BEFORE WE GO OVER TO THE RINGSIDE, LET ME JUST TELL YOU ABOUT SKWEEKY WEETS!
WHAT? WE WANT TO SEE THE FIGHT!

...THE SKWEEKIEST WEET WITH THE WEETIEST SKWEEK...
SKWEEKY WEETS
THIS IS AN OUTRAGE!

SKWEEKY WEETS
BUT DON'T JUST TAKE MY WORD FOR IT! LISTEN TO THE TESTIMONY OF A SATISFIED CUSTOMER...
??
EEK!
THEY'RE THE SKWEEKIEST!
IS THIS YOUR DOING?
NO! IT'S NOT ME! IT'S ANOTHER CARTOON CAT IN A MASK!
IT IS YOUR DOING!
SKWEEKY SKWEEKY SKWEEKY
IT'S JUST THAT... EVERY TIME I LOOK AT A TELLY IT'S GOT AN ADVERT FOR SKWEEKY WEETS ON IT....
OK! OK! I'M GOING!

MY AFFLICTION... MY BURDEN... MY MISERY...
BONG

A CUP OF TEA...
TOMS TEA

LOOK AT THIS! MY NEW PHONE APP PICKS UP DIGITAL TV STATIONS!
WOW!
COOL!

?
HEY! WHAT'S THIS? IT SHOULDN'T DO THIS!
...SKWEEKY WEETS...

TOM'S
IT'S OK NOW!
HE HAD SOMETHING TO DO WITH IT!

YEAH! IT'S THAT CAT... WHAT'S HIS NAME!
THE ONE WITH THE GRIN...

TOM'S TEA
OW! OW! SORRY SORRY SORRY...
...AND I'M STILL HUNGRY! I'LL BUY A SNACK...

PACKET OF CRISPS, PLEASE...
SORRY, I'VE RUN OUT!
LE SNACK SHOP
OH... QUAVERS?
RUN OUT OF THEM TOO...
GOT A KITKAT?
NO
TOPIC?
NO
YORKIE?
NO
SHERBET DIPDAB?
HANG ON A MINUTE... NO
FREDDO?
NO
BISCUIT GALAXY?
NO
PACKET OF POLOS?
NO
WELL, WHAT HAVE YOU GOT?
THE ONLY THING I'VE GOT LEFT, SIR, IS THIS NEW CEREAL BAR...
I'LL TAKE IT! CHARGE IT TO MY ESTATE! I MUST DASH...
SNACKS

I HAVE A HORRIBLE FEELING...
I KNEW IT! AAAAARGH!!
SKWEEKY WEETZ BAR

KILL!!
AH, BOSS! YOU'RE JUST IN TIME FOR...

AN EPISODE OF ADAM ADAMANT, STARRING GERALD HARPER!

AW.... GREAT!
ADAM ADAMANT! ADAM ADAMANT

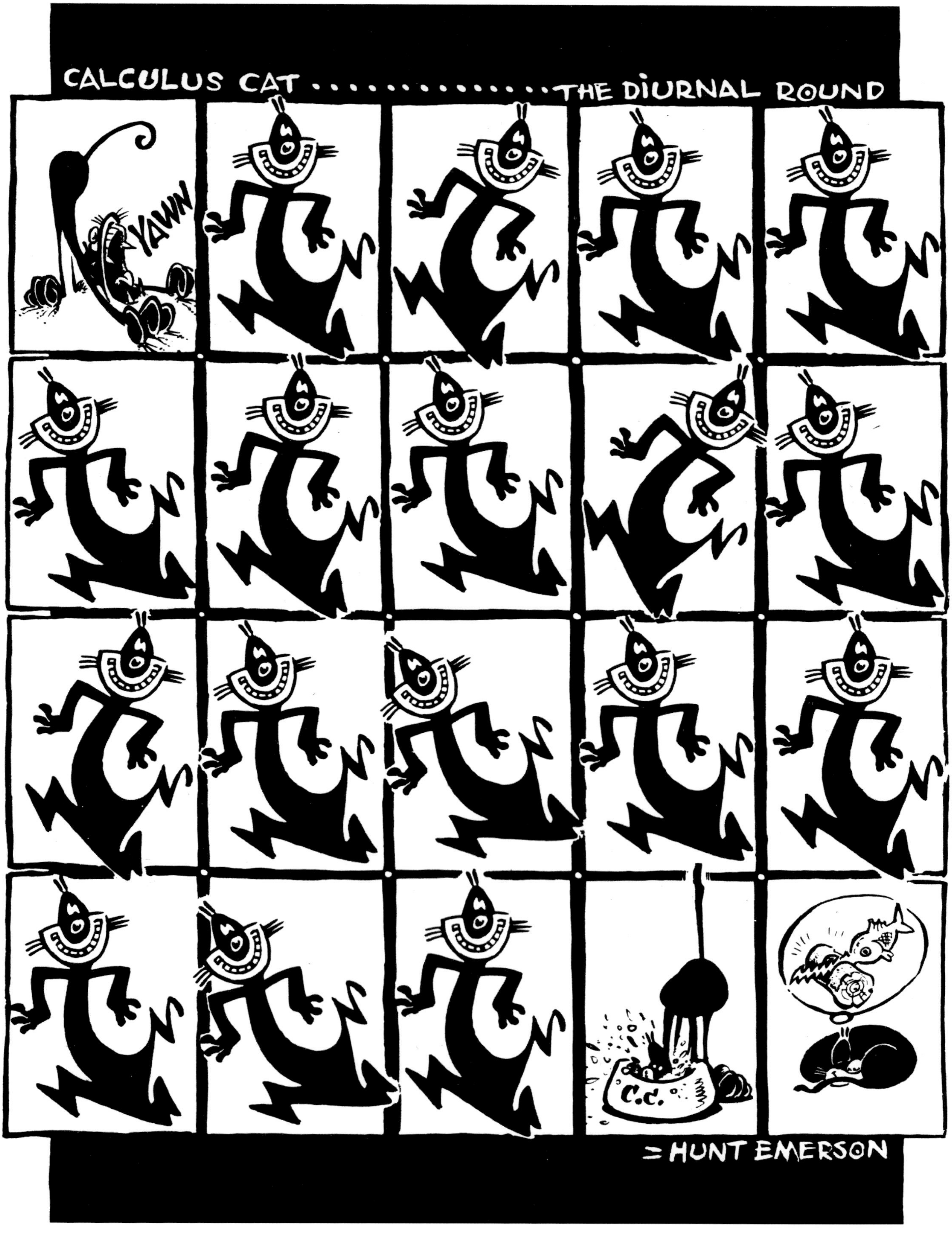

CALCULUS CAT .... THE DIURNAL ROUND

YAWN

C.C.

= HUNT EMERSON

THE CALCULUS CAT GALLERY

I am proud and delighted to present these versions of Calculus Cat drawn by some of my favourite cartoonists, ranging from veteran Gilbert Shelton to neophyte Kitet Hommelhoff, and taking in many of the world's finest in between. I hope you like them all as much as I do!

This page: Graham Higgins, UK.
Right: Rian Hughes, UK.

WOSS ON THE TELLY?
CALCULUS CAT

This page:
Phil Elliott, UK.
Kate Charlesworth, UK.
Right: Keith Burn, UK.

This page: Gary Northfield, UK.
Kev F. Sutherland, UK.
Right: Kevin O'Neill, UK.
Marcatti, Brazil.

TV BUMF 3D Special
WELCOME
O'Neill

FROM BRAZIL
30.6.2014

This page:
Max, Spain.
Paul Wardle, Canada.
Right:
Laura Howell, UK.

SKWEEKY WEETS
NOW SKWEEKIER!
SKWEEKY WEETS
NOW WEETIER!

This page: Suzy Varty, UK.
Graham Higgins, UK.
Right: Dave McKean, UK.

This page: Ste Pickford, UK.
Kitet Hommelhoff, Australia.
Right: Graham Higgins, UK.
(after Edvard Munch, Norway.)

This page: Tim Leatherbarrow, UK.
Right: Hurricane Ivan, Italy.

MEOW
!
HURRICANE for HUNT!

Skweeky Weets
KA14

This page: Lew Stringer, UK.
Left: Krent Able, UK.

ROGER LANGRIDGE 2014

Left: Roger Langridge, UK.
This page: Juba, Finland.

This page: Steve Gibson, UK.
Right: Jon Berkeley, Spain.

SKWEEKY WEETS
Hooray for
CALCULUS CAT
NOW IN
STRETCHYSCOPE
JON BERKELEY
AFTER
HUNT EMERSON

This page: Gabby Noble, UK.
Right: John McCrea, UK.

ROY CONOLLY

This page: Gilbert Shelton, France.
Steve Pugh, UK.
Left: Roy Conolly, UK.

skweek
CHRIS WELCH

Left: Chris Welch, Australia.
This page: Andy 'Doodles' Baker, UK.
Brick, UK.

YEEK! SKWEEKY-WEETS TWEETS!!!
BRIGHTY FOR HUNT.

This page: Eric Knisley, USA.
Rich Stone, UK.
Left: Steve Bright, UK.

CALCULUS IS RUDELY WOKEN FROM HIS HOLIDAY SLUMBER... IS NO WHERE SAFE FROM THE TV IN 21ST CENTURY?
BEN

Both pages: Ben Hunt, UK.

THAT'S IT-
THE END!

NOW - LESSEE WOSSONNER TELLY?